Wellington and Kevin are very sad. They have nowhere to live. Their kennel has gone. The rain has taken it far away.

They go to the garden. They sit by the rhubarb and look at the plants. They bark at the starlings when they fly to the ground.

Then it starts to rain. Kevin and Wellington hide under the rhubarb, but they get wet. "We need somewhere to live," says Wellington.

Soon Kevin is hungry. The two dogs go to look for their dishes. They find them in the farmyard. They are empty. The pigs have eaten their food.

Then it goes dark. The stars sparkle in the night sky. The moon comes out from behind a cloud. Kevin looks very sad in the moonlight.

The clouds come over the moon and the stars. It starts to rain. Kevin and Wellington hide under the rhubarb again. They get wet again.

"I wish we were in our kennel," says Kevin. "Do you think it is far away? Can we go to look for it tomorrow?"

The next day the two dogs go to look for their kennel. They look far and wide, but they cannot find it. They go slowly back to the farm.

As they come to the farmyard gate, they see something new. It is a smart new kennel. It has "GUARD DOGS" written on it. "Is it for us?" asks Kevin.

Yes. The smart new kennel is for Wellington and Kevin. They have a new home. They feel very proud as they guard all the animals in the farmyard.

"ar"

are	far
garden	rhubarb
bark	starlings
starts	farmyard
dark	stars
sparkle	farm
smart	guard